Series title: BLACK LEADERS IN THE FREEDOM
STRUGGLE

MARY

SEACOLE

by Marie Stuart

Illustrated by Folake Shoga

This book is part of a series written by Marie Stuart (Tyrwhitt) and published in her memory.

Marie wanted stories about the lives of these brave people to be more widely known. She believed that such stories would serve to encourage those facing the same challenges today.

Published in 1993 by Central and East Bristol Adult Continuing Education©, with the sponsorship of relatives, friends and colleagues of Marie Tyrwhitt.

First reprint 1995
Second reprint 1999

Marie Tyrwhitt Publications© c/o Dr Charles Claxton, Community Education Centre, Stoke Lodge, Shirehampton Road, Bristol BS9 1BN.

Printed by University of the West of England, Bristol Printing and Stationery Services.

Marie Stuart, the author of the books in the Black Leaders in the Freedom Struggle series, was a teacher of adults and children and a writer throughout all her long life. She was also a learner and one who believed that to be really alive means to be growing and changing. To do so means that we must be free. Free to question and free to find our own answers and our own way.

Marie Stuart wrote these books out of a passion for freedom for all, regardless of race, colour or creed, and out of a deep admiration for the heroes celebrated in this series. They are 'heroes' not because they conquered great empires, but because, by their actions and their example, they gave something of great value to the liberation of their people. They stood up and took their place proudly amongst the human race, having struggled heroically against the disadvantages to which they were born. These stories and those lives will never die as long as we have the courage to strive for our human right to dignity and equality and the generosity to realise that the breath of freedom is sharing. It is in that spirit that these books should be read and in loyalty to the memory of those brave black leaders in our freedom struggle.

MARY SEACOLE

Chapter 1
Mary Learns to be a 'Doctress'

Most people have heard of Florence Nightingale and her nursing in the Crimea. However, there is another woman who should be known and honoured by everyone with equal, if not more acclaim, and her name is Mary Seacole. She wrote a book about her life, and this story is based on what she tells of her "wonderful adventures".

She was born in Kingston, Jamaica, in the year 1805. Her name then was Mary Grant. She had a brother named Edward and a sister Louisa. Her mother was a black Jamaican, and her father, who came from Scotland, was white. So Mary was a Creole.

Her father was an army officer and seems to have been away with the army most of the time, so Mary saw very little of him. Her mother kept a boarding-house, which was also a kind of nursing home. In those days two English regiments, the 97th and the 48th, were camped in Jamaica at Uptown, near Kingston. Many of the soldiers' wives went to stay with Mary's mother when they had their babies, or if they were ill. Some of the officers from the regiments went there too if they were sick. Mrs. Grant was a clever nurse, or "doctress" as she was called. She knew a lot about herbs and could often cure the men better than the white army doctors could. When Horatio Nelson was a young man, before he became a Lord, she nursed him back to health from a very bad fever.

When Mary was a child she loved to play with pet cats and dogs, pretending they were sick. She does not say in her book if she ever went to school, but she knew how to read and write. She was also quick with sums and making sure that she had the right change when she went shopping for her mother. However by the time that she was twelve, she thought she was too old for playing. Every day she was helping her mother look after the sick people. She also learned how to cook, for Mrs. Grant knew that people need good food to help them get well.

As Kingston is a port in Jamaica, Mary used to see the ships coming and going in the harbour. She often wished that she could sail away in one of them and, when she was about twenty, her dream came true. She went to England with some of her father's people and was there for about a year. At first she was upset because some of the boys in the London streets made fun of the colour of her skin. But that did not stop her from making another journey there the next year. This time she took a large stock of Jamaican jams and pickles with her and sold them for a good price. She was a good business woman.

Back in Jamaica again she lived with her mother helping her and learning all she could from her. One of the sick men who was being looked after by them was named Edwin Horatio Seacole. He was the god-son of Horatio Nelson whom Mary's mother had cured of the fever. He fell in love with Mary and they were married on November 10th, 1836. Sadly he did not live many years in spite of Mary's loving care. Soon afterwards, her mother also died, and she was left alone "to battle with the world as best she could." It was no easy thing in those days for a widow to manage on her own. To make matters worse, there was the Great Fire in Kingston in 1843, and the boarding-house which her mother had left her was burned down.

Yet Mary was never one to accept defeat without putting up a good fight. "Of course, I set to work again in a humbler way, and rebuilt my house by degrees and restocked it, better than before", she wrote in her book. By this time everyone knew what a good nurse she was and her house was always full of sick officers and their wives. Sometimes she had a naval or military surgeon under her roof, and she learned a lot from them. Once, when there was an outbreak of cholera in Kingston, a doctor lodging in her house gave her many hints as to the best treatment for this terrible disease. What she learned from him helped her to save many lives, not only then, but in the future.

Kingston, Jamaica

Chapter 2
Business Venture in Panama

Mary was now forty-five and she felt time was passing. Her brother, Edward, had left Jamaica and gone to set up a store and hotel in Panama. Why should she not join him? Her sister, Louisa, could look after the boarding-house in Kingston while she was away. It would be good to have a change. Having made up her mind, she did not let any grass grow under her feet. She set to work busily, for she was not going empty-handed. "My house was full for weeks," she wrote, "making up rough coats and trousers etc., and seamstresses cutting out and making shirts. My kitchen was filled with busy people making jams and pickles."

All these things she planned to take with her for her brother's store. She also took a little girl to help her, and a manservant named Mac. They went by steamer to Navy Bay and then by rail to Panama. This was before the Panama canal had been cut across the narrow strip of land that joins North to South America. In those days it was a terrible place where fever, ague, and dropsy were rampant. Because of the heavy rain the ground was swampy. There were no good roads and the railway lines ran on piles driven into the mud. You might ask why anyone wanted to go there. The answer was to try to find gold. Because of the Gold Rush to California, men came from all over the world hoping to be one of the lucky ones to find it. The life was hard, and so were the men, and the few women who went with them. It was not at all as Mary had pictured it.

To get to Chagres, where her brother had his store, she had to hire a boat and get all her luggage on board with the help of Mac and the little girl, who was also called Mary. It was raining all the time and the river was flooded. Twice they had to get out of one boat and into another, and that meant climbing up and down steep banks, slippery with red mud. Mary, who wanted to look her best when she met her brother, was wearing a pretty pale blue dress, a white shawl and a white bonnet trimmed with blue ribbon. Before long she was covered with red mud and her clothes ruined!

When she met Edward on the wharf she was very angry. "Why did you ask me to come to this horrible place?" she scolded. "Look at the state I am in, cold, hungry, and wretched! I want to wash and change and have something to eat."

However, the place was so full of noisy, wild people that there was no room to do even this! And that night she, and little Mary, had to sleep on the floor under the table in the main room, while her brother and Mac slept on top!

Next day was a bit better when some of the crowd moved on. At once Mary began to set up a hotel of her own, but before she could get started there was an outbreak of cholera. There were no doctors in Chagres, but Mary had her medicine chest with her - she never went anywhere without it. She was able to save the life of her first patient, and this good news spread as rapidly as the disease. Mary worked day and night to save as many lives as she could. Some of her patients were rich and they paid her very well. Others had no money, but she helped them all, rich and poor alike. She tried to teach them that they could help themselves by clearing the filth and mud from their huts and the streets. In the end, she herself went down with an attack, but fortunately it was a mild one.

Even when the cholera was over, her skill as a nurse and 'doctress' was called upon every day. There were frequent fights between the gold prospectors, gamblers and muleteers. Stabbings gave her plenty of practice in attending to knife wounds, torn ears and so on. So she was able to make good use of what the surgeon had taught her when he stayed at the boarding-house in Kingston.

In the end, she did open a store and hotel of her own, not far away from her brother. But she was not really happy there - the life was so rough and wild. She stuck it for about three years and then made up her mind to go back home to Jamaica. At Navy Bay she bought tickets for herself, little Mary and Mac on an American ship. But the white women passengers were so disgustingly rude to them because of the colour of their skin that she changed to an English ship instead. At that time there was still slavery in America and white people would not travel with black. Many English people were just as bad, but there were others who were working for the abolition of slavery. As for Mary, she herself did not pay attention to the colour of a person's skin. Perhaps the fact that she had a black mother and a white father gave her this wisdom. To her a man was a man, a woman a woman, black or white, rich or poor, and if they needed help, she gave it. Because she respected herself, insults could hurt her but did not prevent her from doing what she felt to be right.

Mary got back to Jamaica just in time to help nurse the victims of a terrible epidemic of yellow fever. Her boarding-house, which had been kept going by her sister, was soon full of patients, many of whom sadly died. One young officer, of whom she was very fond, died in her arms. Later, his mother wrote Mary a letter, from England, thanking her for her loving care and sending her a brooch with a lock of the young man's hair in it. Mary was very upset by this young man's death and by his will in which he left his dog to one friend, his ring to another, and "kind wishes to all." Later, this same young man's brother was able to help Mary in the Crimea.

Chapter 3
Rebuff from Florence Nighingale

When the yellow fever epidemic was over, Mary made a short trip back to Panama to wind up the affairs of the hotel she had set up there. A relative of hers named Mr. Day went with her, and they became business partners. She did not return to Jamaica as she had intended because she heard that England had declared war against Russia and that fighting had started in the Crimea. Very few people knew where the Crimea was, but Mary found an old map and made a red cross to mark the spot. Constantinople (now called Istanbul) was a name she kept seeing in the papers and this seemed to be the place where the fighting was going on. She remembered her father who had been an officer and knew that if he were still alive he would have been there. She felt his blood flowing through her veins and longed to join one of the regiments to go and see for herself and help if she could. But she was a woman, what could she do? She decided that the first thing was to go to England to find out. So she booked her passage at Navy Bay and set off. All the way on the voyage she was planning what to do. She had read in the newspaper that the regiments of the 97th and 68th were fighting in the Crimea. Both these regiments had been stationed in Jamaica for three years and she had nursed many of the officers, men, and their wives through cholera, dysentery, yellow fever, etc., so she knew that she would have a lot of friends in their ranks. Some of them would be able to help her and tell her what to do.

She got to London in the autumn of 1854, just after the Battle of Alma. The first thing she did was to apply to the War Office for the post of a hospital nurse, enclosing a glowing testimonial from a Medical Officer she had known in Jamaica - but she had no reply. Then she tried to get an interview with the Secretary at War and other "high-ups," but they ignored her. When she heard of Florence Nightingale's band of nurses she tried to join them but was told there was no room for her. Why? Why? Was it because she was not white? She was so upset at the injustice of this that she broke down and cried in the open street with the unheeding crowd jostling past her. Standing there alone she closed her eyes in prayer, begging God to show her the way.

There is a saying, "God helps those who help them-selves." Mary Seacole not only *said* this, she *believed* it. If no-one would help her get to the Crimea, she would go on her own, paying her own way. She knew that, once there, she would meet officers and "high-up" army men, perhaps even a general, as well as doctors who had known her in Jamaica. She was sure they would help her. Her plan was to open a hotel for invalids and wounded in the Crimea, similar to the one she had had in Kingston. She would call it "British Hotel." She would use her own money to get it going - luckily she had enough from the sale of her hotel in Panama. There was no time to be lost.

She had cards printed and posted them off to as many of her army friends as she could think of. She knew they would be stationed in the Crimea at Sebastopol and that these cards would let them know she was on her way. The next thing was to book her passage to Balaclava. This done, and while she was waiting for the sailing date, she met Mr. Day, her relative, who was also in London on business. He was going to Balaclava ahead of her but they decided to go into partnership again. They planned to open up a store and hotel near the army camp before Sebastopol under their joint names of Seacole and Day. He then left and Mary spent most of her time and money on stocking up with medicines and "home comforts" till the day came for her departure.

Her ship docked at Malta on the way out and there she was able to meet some doctors she had known in Jamaica. One of them had just come from the Crimea and gave her a letter of introduction to Florence Nightingale who was then in charge of the military hospital at Scutari, near Constantinople. This was where most of the wounded were sent from the battle-front.

Her next stop was at Constantinople where she picked up a letter from Mr. Day telling her what other things she should buy. She then hired a small boat to take her to the hospital at Scutari to meet Florence Nightingale. As she walked through the wards of the hospital, some of the wounded men recognised her and cried out, "Mother Seacole!" begging her to come over to their bedsides. They were so comforted to see her and hoped she would be staying to help nurse them.

Finally she was able to see Florence Nightingale herself. She greeted Mary politely, but without warmth, and showed no interest in her plans. Nor did she arrange for Mary to be conducted round the hospital so that she could meet again some of the men she had known from the old days. Since both women were pioneers in nursing it would have seemed natural for them to have had many things in common to discuss. Unfortunately this did not happen. Miss Nightingale made Mary feel that she was too busy to give up more of her time. As the weather had turned stormy and the sea was too rough for an immediate return journey, arrangements were made for Mary to stay the night. As there was no room in the nurses' quarters, she had to sleep with the hospital washer-women. She said that she enjoyed the company of the washer-women, who were friendly and welcoming, but not that of the fleas in her bed! Mary made no comment on the lack of friendship shown to her by "the Lady of the Lamp." Anyway, she was eager to get started on her own plans.

Chapter 4
Setting up Store in Spring Hill

She did not wish to stay in Constantinople but was set to go on to Balaclava where the fighting was taking place. She was not put off by Mr. Day's letters telling her of the bad conditions there. So she hired a local boy to help her with the shopping she needed to do for the store they were to set up. Then she booked a passage on a boat to cross the Black Sea to Balaclava. The harbour was crowded with shipping of all shapes and sizes. Mr. Day met her at the wharf. They had to unload all their stores on the quay-side and protect them from the weather and thieves as well as they were able.

Next day she sent off more letters to her friends to tell them of her arrival. They all wrote back very kindly and some of them came to welcome her. She even got the Port-Admiral to delay the sailing of one of his ships because some of her stores had been loaded on it by mistake and were in danger of being sent back to Constantinople! At first he raged at her and grumbled about a parcel of women coming out where they were not wanted, but when she told him that she had once nursed his son in Jamaica, he relented. Later, when he saw her working with the wounded on the wharf, he came up to her and clapped her on the shoulder, saying, "Glad to see you here, old lady, among these poor fellows!" and she saw there was a tear-drop in his eye. He was one person in authority who respected her for her bravery and courage.

She spent six weeks in Balaclava on the wharf, partly attending to her stores and selling some in a tarpaulin tent she had rigged up to protect them from the rain and wind. She slept at night over a barrel of gunpowder on one of the ammunition ships anchored alongside. To get on deck she had to climb up the ship's side by means of a perilous ladder - many times she nearly had a ducking!

Tired as she was at the end of the day, she often made sponge cakes and lemonade on board ship as the poor soldiers said they liked them "more than anything, because they tasted of home." Home was what they all longed for. Some of those who were dying of their wounds mistook her for their mother or wife, and she held them in her arms to the end to comfort them. No woman ever had as many "sons" as "Mother Seacole."

Most of the time she helped the doctors move the wounded men from the mules or horse-drawn carts to the ships that would take them across the Black Sea to the Florence Nightingale hospital at Scutari. She re-

"She was Mother Seacole, a loving human being."

bandaged their wounds and brought them cups of tea for their parched lips. But, no matter how busy she was, she did not forget her looks and liked to wear her best yellow dress and blue bonnet. Not for her the prim dark uniform and stiff white apron and cap of Florence Nightingale's nurses! She was Mother Seacole, a loving human being, and the men could feel that she really *cared* for them. They were not just casualties, but each one of them was someone's son, brother or lover and mattered to that person, and to her.

At last the plans for the setting up of the store of Seacole and Day were ready. They settled upon a spot about two miles from Balaclava, called Spring Hill. They collected wood from the wrecks in the harbour, with permission of the old admiral, and hired men to build the sheds. The best workers were two English sailors she nicknamed Big and Little Chips. There was also a Turkish officer she nicknamed Ali Baba, who gave her four windows and a glass door which he had got from a village his company had occupied.

Every day she went to Spring Hill to see how things were going on, sometimes on horseback, sometimes by mule, sometimes in one of the horse-and-cart "ambulances." The hotel and store-room was an oblong hut with shelves, cupboards, and counters inside. There was another storey above it which was used for storing goods, and on the roof they set up a pole to fly the Union

Jack. On the first floor they had a kitchen where a great deal of cooking was done, and there was a canteen beside it. There were also out-houses for the servants to sleep in and two small bedrooms, one for Mary and the other for Mr. Day.

They also had a large yard with stables, sheds and sties, for they kept horses, mules, pigs, and fowls. Indeed the saying went that you could get everything at Mother Seacole's "from an anchor down to a needle." In addition they had four carts and as many horses and mules as they could keep from the thieves. The worst thieves of their food were the rats!

Mary could always see the funny side of things, even when they went against her. She tells how one night her best horse was stolen and the only one left in the stable was an old grey mare with bare patches in her coat. That day she needed to ride over to the French camp but was ashamed to be seen on the back of such an animal. What could she do? A bright idea came to her - to cover the bald places with flour so that they would not show. That seemed to do the trick, so off she set. But alas! it was a very windy day and her cloak kept blowing against the animal's sides so that the flour was rubbed off leaving the bald patches on the mare as before. When she got to the camp everyone could see what had happened and she was greeted with a roar of laughter in which she joined as heartily as anyone.

Chapter 5
Mother Seacole - Storekeeper, Friend and Nurse

It was not only the battle wounds which needed Mary's care. Many of the soldiers were now suffering from cholera, dysentery, jaundice and diarrhoea. The herbal remedies she had learned about from her mother were very useful in curing these sicknesses and her book contains many letters from thankful patients she had nursed back to health. Those who could afford to pay her did so, but, to quote her own words, she could not charge herself "with doing less for the man who has only his thanks to give." One of the generals wrote about her that she not only looked after the wounded in places of great danger, but "in addition kept a very good store and supplied them with comforts at a time when they most needed them."

They used to roast twenty or so fowls daily, killed and plucked in their own yard, besides boiling hams, tongues, and a side of beef or mutton. She had a few servants, mostly Turks, and two black cooks, but she did quite a lot of the cooking herself. Whenever she had a few spare moments she used to wash her hands, roll up her sleeves, and make pastry. Very often she was interrupted to dispense medicines, but "if the tarts had a flavour of senna and the puddings tasted of rhubarb it never interfered with their consumption." Indeed the officers would crowd into her little kitchen and carry off the tarts hot from the oven. She said they made her frantic and she would sometimes rap their greedy fingers with a spoon to stop them. Rice pudding was a great favourite with the men, because it made them think of home. "What a shout there used to be," she wrote, "when I came out of my little caboose, hot and flurried, and called out, 'Rice pudding today, my sons!'"

Yes, she looked upon them all as her sons and sorrowed like a mother for them when they were killed. But while they lived she did her best to make life as happy and comfortable as possible for them. Even a little thing like the lack of a handkerchief did not escape her notice! One day she asked a young officer to give her his handkerchief so that she could wrap something up for him in it as paper was scarce. He told her he had torn up an old shirt a fortnight ago to make some but had none left now. So what did she do? Sent in an order to Constantinople for a hundred dozen handkerchiefs and sold them all in next to no time to the men who came to her store. In addition to her other skills, Mary was a good business woman!

21

She was also very brave and frequently attended wounded men in situations of great danger. Far from running away from the battlefield she was often "under fire." Of her first experience of an actual battle she wrote, "I felt a strange excitement - coupled with an earnest longing to see more of warfare, and to share in its hazards." It was not long before her wish was fulfilled. The night before the French attacked the Russians at the Redan she had a hunch that something unusual was afoot. She did not go to bed at her usual time but walked to a hill three and a half miles away and saw many regiments making their way down into the trenches ready to attack the Russians at dawn. She stayed watching till midnight, then walked back to Spring Hill and woke her helpers to prepare for the next day, cutting sandwiches, packing up ham, fowls, tongue etc.

She herself filled her bag, which she always carried over her shoulder, with bandages, lint, needles and thread and medicines. They packed everything on two mules and set off for the battle scene. At first they were stopped by sentries from entering the battle-zone, but when they heard who it was they let her pass. She made her way to a spot where the hospital tent had been put up and helped the doctors with the wounded. She was the only woman there. When the soldiers heard a shell coming overhead they would shout, "Lie down, mother! Lie down!" As she was rather stout it was not easy for her to

get up again and often one of the men would come to give her a hand. Once she fell on her hand and put her thumb out of joint, but she stayed all day looking after the wounded and did not get back to Spring Hill until late that night. The battle of Redan was a terrible defeat for the French and it was followed by an armistice.

Chapter 6
End of the War

During the lull there was an outbreak of cholera of which many died, including the British Commander-in-Chief. Mary was busy nursing the victims but she also found time to restock the British Hotel "with every conceivable necessity of life." Wisely she planned ahead for she knew that there would be fighting again soon. Indeed there was another great battle, and once again she was there helping whoever was in need, not only English soldiers, but their allies the French and Sardinians - and even the enemy Russians. One of these gave her a ring from his finger as he lay dying and kissed her hand. All thanked her, even if she could not understand the words, with a smile - "the common language of all the world".

Finally the fighting ended on September 8th with the fall of Sebastopol and the defeat of the Russians. Of course the English newspapers were full of the news. *The Times* spoke about the part Mrs. Seacole had played in caring for the wounded in these words:

"... once again she was there, helping whoever
was in need"

"I saw her at the assault on the Redan, at Tchernaya and at the fall of Sebastopol, laden, not with plunder, good old soul, but with wine, bandages, and food for the wounded or the prisoners!"

Afterwards she went into the ruins of Sebastopol and saw the terrible sights in the hospital where thousands were lying dead or dying. Many of the soldiers were drunk and playing wild pranks. They were looting from the shops and houses. One of them offered Mary half of a grand piano! She refused it, but brought away an old teapot and a parasol as souvenirs.

From September till Christmas, when the peace treaty was signed, the troops stayed on as the Russians retreated. After all the hardship, danger and pain they had put up with for months, all they wanted now was to get back home as soon as possible, and, in the meantime, to have fun with dancing, dinner parties, gambling and all kinds of amusements. Some of the English and Russian soldiers became friends, for, as Mary says, "War, like death, is a great leveller, and mutual suffering and endurance has made us all friends."

Of course, the end of the war meant the end of the British Hotel. Mary had bought large supplies of articles and food which were no longer needed and for which there was no sale. She could not take it back to England, so she had to let it go "dirt cheap" to the Russians who came to buy and plunder. She smashed dozens of bottles of wine rather than let them have it for nothing. When she finally got back to England she was far poorer than when she left, and the firm of Seacole and Day went bankrupt.

She did not want to go back to Jamaica and she had no home in London, but she had many friends. "Where indeed do I not find them?" she wrote, "In omnibuses, in river steam-boats, in places of public amusement, in quiet streets and courts, where taking short cuts, I lose my way oft-times. Old familiar faces spring up to remind me of the months spent on Spring Hill."

Very soon a fund was set up to help her out of her money problems. His Royal Highness, the Prince of Wales, was the Patron, and many "high-ups" in the army were on the committee. Thanks to the generous response to "the fund" she was able to live in comfort, but her health and energy were never the same after all the hardships she had put up with in the Crimea. She did not travel again but lived mostly in, or near, London. She died at the ripe old age of seventy-six and was buried in St. Mary's Catholic Cemetery, Harrow Road, London.

Series title:
BLACK LEADERS IN THE FREEDOM STRUGGLE

Titles published:

Sojourner Truth

Frederick Douglass

Josiah Henson

Harriet Tubman

Booker Washington

Marcus Garvey

Toussaint L'Ouverture

The Wonderful Adventures of Mrs Seacole

Paul Robeson

Martin Luther King

and an introduction: Slavery in America